Everything
You Need to
Know About

Down
Syndrome

Kids with Down syndrome are much like everyone else—but not all kids with DS are alike.

Everything You Need to Know About

Down Syndrome

Mary Bowman-Kruhm, Ed.D.

Rosen Publishing Group, Inc./New York

*To the members of downsyn@listserv.nodak.edu, whose e-mail posts
provide support to families who have a member with Down syndrome,
and information on DS to the worldwide Internet community.*

Thanks to Rick Dill, who provided not only quotes but insight on having an adult child with DS, and to Amy Masser, who graciously spent several hours sharing information with me about Katy, her daughter with Down syndrome.

Very special thanks to Dr. Len Leshin, who readily agreed to review this book and whose thoughtful comments much improved it.

Thank you to the National Association for Down Syndrome (NADS) for its review of the manuscript.

Published in 2000 by The Rosen Publishing Group, Inc.
29 East 21st Street, New York, NY 10010

First Edition

Library of Congress Cataloging-in-Publication Data

Bowman-Kruhm, Mary.
    Everything you need to know about Down syndrome / Mary Bowman-Kruhm.
      p. cm. — (The need to know library)
    Includes bibliographical references and index.
    Summary: Examines causes of Down syndrome, new developments in
medical treatment, and changes in attitudes toward people who have this condition.
    ISBN 0-8239-2949-3
    1. Down syndrome Juvenile literature. 2. Mental retardation Juvenile literature.
[1. Down syndrome. 2. Mentally handicapped.] I. Title. II. Series.
    RJ506.D68B68 1999
    616.85'8842—dc21   99-32465
                                                     CIP
                                                        AC

Contents

Introduction

"**H**alf the kids at school tell me how dumb my sister is and call her a sped." Daryl looked straight at his mother as he spoke. "And your friends . . . they all say how lovable she is."

"Your sister is not dumb. Susan does have problems with schoolwork. But she can do lots of things very well indeed. And the term 'sped' should not be used to describe anyone." Daryl's mother smiled and sipped from her cup of tea.

"Well, she's sure not always lovable!" Daryl said.

"Maybe not always," his mother agreed. "But she has individual qualities all her own. Just like anyone else."

"Down syndrome," or DS for short, is a term that most often is used to describe someone born with the special characteristics, or traits, that are associated with the condition.

If you know someone with Down syndrome or if you just want to know more about it, this book is for you. You will find out why some babies are born with Down syndrome. Because DS is characterized by serious medical, learning, and other problems, this book will tell you about some of the challenges faced by people with DS. It also will describe the ways in which people with DS can improve their skills in coping with life, and how family and friends can help them grow into valuable members of a community.

Children with Down syndrome
need special attention.

Chapter One

What Is Down Syndrome?

Katie was born with Down syndrome. At age two, she is just beginning to walk. Her older brother worries when she walks on his bed; he is afraid that she will fall. Her mother feels that Katie's mental abilities are more advanced than her physical coordination. Katie is able to use some words to let her family know what she wants. If she cannot think of the word, she uses hand signs. When the purple dinosaur on television starts to dance and sing, Katie loves to join in. She seems to understand, but she must lean against the sofa when she dances.

Jeb, who is two years old and was born with Down syndrome, "combat crawls," with his weight on his elbows and his legs trailing behind his body.

When he really wants to move quickly, he rolls. Jeb has babbled since he was a few months old. Now he can say, "dog," "mama," and "dada." When he wants a bottle, he says, "ba-ba." When his big brother tries to feed him, Jeb wants to feed himself. His overall health is good.

Erin is a two-year-old who was born with Down syndrome. She has a heart problem that required surgery when she was only five months old. She is on her third set of tubes in her ears (for persistent ear infections) and wears a hearing aid. The fluid that builds up in her ears when she gets an infection is a problem because it affects her speech, hearing, and balance. She does not respond to noises and yanks at her hearing aid. Erin has just started to sit up without using her hands for support. She gurgles and babbles when she is happy.

Each one of these three children is much like any other toddler. They all need the love and care of their families; they are learning how to make their needs known; they play and like to be played with.

Even though all of these children were born with Down syndrome, they are quite different from each other. Their skills and needs are different. They will continue to grow into very different people as they get older.

How Down Syndrome Was Named

Down syndrome is the name used today to describe babies born with a specific set of special characteristics, or traits. For ease, the name often is shortened to DS.

The syndrome is named after Dr. John Langdon Down, a British doctor who first identified the condition in 1866. The word "syndrome" means that all children with DS share those characteristics that Dr. Down first noted.

The Extra Chromosome

In 1959 Dr. Jerome Lejeune of Paris linked the cause of DS to the presence of an extra chromosome. Our bodies are made up of tiny cells that are too small to be seen except through a microscope. In the center of each cell is a nucleus. Around this nucleus are genetic materials, or genes, that we inherit from our parents. Each nucleus holds about 100,000 genes.

These genes are grouped like beads on a string. Strings of genes are called chromosomes. Normally every baby gets twenty-three chromosomes from each parent. However, babies with DS get an extra twenty-first chromosome from one of their parents. We do not know why.

When there is an extra number twenty-one chromosome, a baby is born with DS. Genes direct how the cells grow and function. In children with DS, the extra genes on the third twenty-first chromosome disrupt growth and the way the cells function. The baby is born smaller and with fewer brain cells. This process begins long before birth and cannot be reversed.

Genetic Forms of DS

Although all individuals with DS have extra chromosome twenty-one material, there are three types of DS.

- Trisomy twenty-one. There is an entire extra chromosome twenty-one in all cells. By far, most cases of DS—95 percent—are this type.

- Translocation. In about 4 percent of cases of DS, the extra twenty-first chromosome material takes the place of part of another chromosome.

- Mosaicism. In about 1 percent of people with DS, an extra whole chromosome is present, but only in some of their cells. Again, doctors do not know exactly why some cells are normal and others are not.

Some of the physical symptoms of DS may be milder in a child with mosaicism, since some of the child's cells are normal. Otherwise all three types are much the same in how they affect a baby born with DS.

Is DS Inherited?

Most cases of DS are not inherited. Mothers or fathers do not cause it. No one can do anything to prevent it.

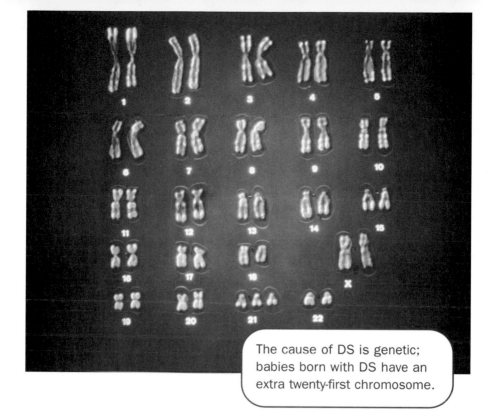

The cause of DS is genetic; babies born with DS have an extra twenty-first chromosome.

Children with DS are born to people of all races, in all countries, to both rich parents and poor. It is not caused by the health or diet of the parents or by anything that a mother does when she is pregnant. It is not a disease, and no one can catch it.

Children with DS account for one out of about every 800 births. The older a mother is, the greater the chance of her having a baby with DS. Since most women have children before age thirty-five, most babies (75 to 80 percent) with DS are born to young mothers.

Features of People with DS

Most babies with DS look much like other members of their family, but they often have some of the distinct physical features, or characteristics, that Dr. Down first noted:

- Eyes that slant upward and outward

- Narrow eye slit

- Face that seems to be flattened

- Small head compared to size of body

- Broad feet with short toes

- Ears that are small and set low on head

- Short arms and legs compared to length of body

- Broad hand with short fingers and a single crease across the palm

- Small mouth that is also small inside and may cause tongue to stick out

- Poor muscle tone

Not everyone with DS has all of these features. If a baby is born with most of them, the doctor orders tests to be sure of the correct diagnosis. Sometimes a baby will have so few of these features that only testing will prove or disprove DS. No matter how many of these features a baby with DS has, no link exists between physical features and intelligence.

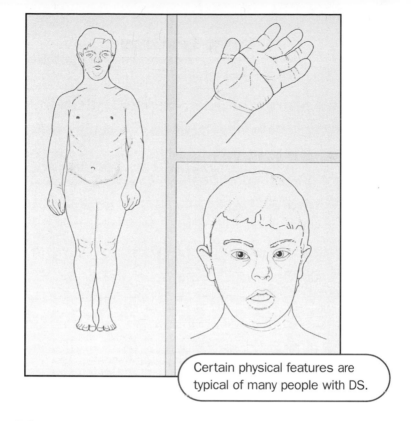

Certain physical features are typical of many people with DS.

Intelligence

Scientists do not know what causes mental retardation. Somehow when the extra chromosome affects cells before birth, the function of the cells in the brain is disturbed. Thus, in standardized tests of intelligence, or IQ tests, children with DS do not score as high as the average child. A lower IQ generally means that someone will have trouble learning in school. Some people with DS have only slightly less trouble doing well in school than the average student; others have a great deal more trouble with intellectual tasks.

You may have heard the terms "mentally retarded," "mentally impaired," and "developmentally delayed" used to refer to someone with DS. These are general

15

terms, widely used to describe a child whose mental and/or physical development and growth is slower than the pace of a typical child. The cause of these delays may have happened at birth, been inherited, or been the result of an injury. The cause may—or may not—be related to an extra chromosome.

Of course, what someone is able to learn in school does not tell us what that person will be able to achieve as an adult. Nor is someone's intelligence, as measured by an IQ test or by one's school performance, a measure of his or her worth as a person. And what someone is able to achieve as an adult—in terms of a career, for example, or financial success—is not the only or the best measurement of what kind of person he or she is.

Chapter Two

At Home During the Early Years

A newborn baby with DS is much like any other baby. He or she cries, likes to be held, probably sleeps a lot, needs to eat often, and uses a lot of diapers. But even though babies with DS are very much like other babies, many have problems that a parent can see—or can look into the future to see.

The truth is that a baby with DS is not always completely welcome at first. Parents soon may become very tired and stressed from providing the extra care their child needs. They may feel cut off from family and friends who do not offer sufficient love and support. Raising a child is never easy; it can be even more difficult when a child has DS.

Stages of Growth

The term "developmental delay" may be used to describe children with DS. Children with DS are often slower, or more delayed, than the average child in developing skills. Most children, for example, walk when they are about a year old. However, a child with DS still may be crawling, scooting on the rump, or rolling to get around at age two. Likewise, other stages of a child's development—smiling, rolling over, sitting, crawling, walking, talking, eating, and dressing—probably will be on a different schedule or calendar for the typical child and for a child with DS. This does not mean that a child with DS will never develop these skills.

Special Health Problems of Children with DS

Several very specific medical problems are linked with DS. Some of the medical problems that people with DS face include thyroid problems; vision problems; muscle, bone, and joint problems; ear, nose, and throat problems; epilepsy; and heart defects.

Thyroid Function
The thyroid is a gland in the neck that produces the thyroid hormone, which helps the body grow and function correctly. When the body does not produce enough

A child with DS may be slower to develop certain skills than the average child, but that does not mean that he or she never will.

thyroid hormone, the resulting condition is called hypothyroidism. Hypothyroidism is the most common thyroid problem for those with DS. It can be present at birth or may occur at any age.

Every state in the United States and many other countries routinely screen all newborns for hypothyroidism, which can be particularly hard to detect in babies with DS because the symptoms resemble many other characteristics an infant with DS might have. Doctors suggest that children with DS be checked for thyroid function at birth, six months of age, one year of age, and then once a year thereafter. Problems with thyroid function usually can be treated well with medication.

Vision Problems

About 70 percent of children with DS have some kind of problem with their vision. Children with DS—like all children—should have their eyes checked at a very young age and then frequently thereafter.

Muscle, Bone, and Joint Problems

Almost all babies with DS have less muscle tone than the average baby. This muscle weakness ranges from mild to severe. Their arms, legs, and neck may be floppy. The child may sit or lie with his or her legs tucked in strange positions. Lack of muscle tone makes the child tire easily. But by the time a child with DS reaches age ten, muscle tone is seldom still a problem.

Some children with DS suffer from what is known as atlanto-axial instability, or AAI. What this means is that they have a large space between their upper vertebrae, which are the segments of the spinal cord. Children with DS should have neck X-rays to check for this problem.

It is not necessary for sports and other physical activities to be limited for children with DS, however, because of bone and joint problems. In some cases, certain precautions need to be taken. Children with DS should take special care to wear all of the correct safety equipment for whatever physical activity they are taking part in.

Although kids with DS sometimes have muscle, bone, and joint problems, they still can play all kinds of sports.

Ear, Nose, and Throat Problems

Particularly tiny air passages in the ears, nose, and throat make some children with DS more likely to have colds, sinus infections, allergies, asthma, and related problems. Consistent monitoring by an ear, nose, and throat specialist is important. Such problems also can lead to problems with sleeping. Sometimes children with DS sleep better after their tonsils and adenoids have been removed. Children with DS also should be tested for hearing problems and carefully monitored thereafter.

Heart Defects

About 40 percent of all babies born with DS have heart defects. Such cases need to be referred to a pediatric cardiologist, a doctor who specializes in the heart problems of children. Babies with DS should have tests for possible heart problems soon after birth. If the child has any other health problems that are severe enough to require surgery, a heart specialist should be consulted before the operation.

Epilepsy

Epilepsy is the name given to a number of similar medical conditions that affect the way the body's central nervous system works. The result is seizures, of different degrees of intensity, that cause people to lose control of their body and some degree of consciousness, or awareness. A mild seizure might last for only a few seconds; an onlooker may hardly be aware that it happened. Some seizures can last as long as several minutes. The person's body stiffens, and his or her arms and legs jerk. Although this is scary to witness, the person is in no pain while the seizure is taking place.

This does not mean that seizures are not dangerous. People can be injured during seizures—they can fall and hit their head or cut and bruise themselves, for example. Overall, 5 to 10 percent of people with DS have seizures. Adults with DS are more likely to have epilepsy or experience seizures than are children with DS. In most cases, the seizures can be controlled with medicine.

Other Problems

Besides health problems, mental retardation and delays in development cause a number of other problems that can be difficult for children with DS, their families, and their friends to cope with. One of the most difficult of these is speech.

Speech

We use language both to understand the world around us and to make our needs and wants known. Many young people with DS, even if they do not have hearing loss, are slow to speak.

For children with DS, learning to speak can be a long, frustrating process. It can be equally frustrating for their parents and other family members. Like any toddler, the child with DS needs and wants to make his or her needs understood. When the child cannot do so, he or she may grow angry or upset and may act out.

Families can do various things to help make communication easier for a child with DS. A speech pathologist can help families with these issues.

Until the child with DS has a better grasp of verbal communication, many parents use sign language to communicate. When a child wants a glass of milk or would like to go outside or has to use the potty, the sign helps the parent understand. Once the child is able to speak, signing is stopped. Until that time,

Like all children, kids with DS need the loving support of family members.

signing provides the parent with a way to communicate with his or her child.

Some parents feel that signing or using word cards and boards in public can make their children look different from the typical child. They insist that the child learn to speak as soon as possible. As with many other child-rearing choices, the family must decide what is right for them and their child.

Family Support

Family support is important for any child, but it is crucial to the child with DS. Among the most important kinds of support the family must provide is taking care of the child's health needs. The family also must help the child develop a strong sense of identity and self-worth. Since the ability to interact with people begins in the home, the family plays a critical role in helping the child develop necessary social skills, including the ability to set boundaries in interactions with others and to make wise decisions. Although family always plays a huge and important role in the life of a child with DS, ultimately the time comes when the child—like any child—must move beyond the family and out into the world.

Chapter Three

A Good IDEA

I *think that the best thing that I did for my child was to put her in day care that had regular-education kids in it. She was the only child there with a disability. Not only did she learn, but she also taught the teachers, who had been afraid and ignorant about the syndrome.*

—Renee Mozingo,
mother of a child with DS

IDEA

A number of laws in the United States are designed to help citizens with disabilities. One of these is Public Law 94-142 (PL94-142, for short), which was first passed by Congress in 1975. PL94-142 grants to all children with disabilities the right to public education. This law has been amended several times and is now known as the Individuals with Disabilities Education Act, or IDEA.

Through IDEA all states receive federal money with which they must provide a "free, appropriate education" to children with disabilities. This includes children with DS. The word "appropriate" means that the school a child attends has to be the right one for him or her—not necessarily the one a school system wants the child to attend.

Evaluation

Before a special education program and services are provided for a child, he or she must undergo a number of tests. These tests are intended to provide information about an individual child's strengths and needs. The information from the tests is gathered, interpreted, and written up into what is called an evaluation. Based on the evaluation, a team, which includes the child's parents, meets to talk about what program and special services, if any, the child needs to help him or her learn.

Individualized Education Programs (IEPs)

Determining a child's needs is a team decision. If the team feels that a child needs a special program, the law requires the team to draw up an Individualized Educational Program (IEP). The program must be approved by the child's parents and the school system.

For small children the plan is called an Individualized Family Service Plan, or IFSP. A similar plan for adults is called an Individualized Training Program, or ITP, and prescribes job and living skills for adults.

The law requires the IEP (or IFSP or ITP) to be reviewed each year. After the review it can be revised or rewritten. The program must spell out the student's learning strengths and weaknesses, the special services needed, special goals and objectives, a timeline for checking on progress, and the people assigned to carry out this program.

Families often feel overwhelmed at such a meeting. Even so, it is important that family members feel free to ask whatever questions they need to. One good idea is to take notes to the meeting that the family has written on what they want to see happen during the coming year. The wording should be kept simple: "Sue can read only about ten words right now. We want her to be able to read one hundred words by June 1." The family should determine what they think will need to be done to reach each goal and ask the staff what methods they will use to reach those goals.

Otherwise, families should keep an open mind about what the young person is now able to do, both in and out of the classroom. They should listen to the school staff and be ready to share their own views.

Individualized learning helps people with DS to utilize their strengths.

Special Services

Special services are often needed to give the child with DS the best chance for success. In fact, at birth a child with DS becomes eligible for services that can help him or her right away. Such services include:

- Speech therapy. Because many children with DS have small mouths, speech therapists may work on feeding problems or on using sign language if the child cannot say words that allow him or her to communicate clearly.

- Physical therapy. A physical therapist works on motor skills, such as walking and standing, as well as muscle tone, which is often helped by massage.

- Occupational therapy. An occupational therapist works on small motor skills, such as grasping and reaching.

- Mental development. A teacher trained to educate young children with DS can work on a child's skill in understanding concepts (such as big and small, open and closed), shapes, and colors. The teacher also can work on social skills and other areas that impact learning.

School Programs

Until recently, most people did not believe that kids with DS could learn. The result was that many children with DS did not get a good education. After all, why did they need to be educated? When they left school, little was expected of them. They stayed at home or lived in institutions with people who had all types of problems. Those with DS seldom interacted with other people in public.

Today society places more of an emphasis on treating each person with DS as an individual and trying to help him or her live an active, full life—the kind of life that everyone wants. This means that school is as important for the child with DS as for any child.

What Kind of Schooling?

Today the parents of a child with DS have many choices about how their child can be educated. For some, home schooling is best even though their child, under IDEA, may attend a public school. These parents feel that their child is safe under their care at home and that they can tailor learning to the child's particular needs.

For other children a private school or a special program in a public school is needed. There trained staff structure every part of the day to meet each student's needs. As a child gets older, such programs have the benefit of offering direct training in work skills to help the young person get and hold a job.

31

Home schooling is the best learning option for many children with DS.

For many students with learning problems of any type, however, the best program allows them to be included in a regular-education classroom with all kinds of learners, some who may need special help and many who do not. A second teacher or aide trained to provide special help often works in the classroom alongside the primary teacher. A program like this is called inclusion because the student is included in the regular program. Because two trained adults in the classroom jointly offer their skills and know-how, all students benefit from true inclusion programs.

Although some people fear that the inclusion of students who require special help will slow down the progress of other students, this rarely happens. Instead studies have shown that *all* students in such groups make great progress, especially in such areas as self-esteem and social skills. It is believed that by welcoming, accepting, and helping children with special needs, other students feel better about themselves, which improves their own ability to learn.

Inclusion, however, can cause some problems. Teachers may need special training to learn how to help students who learn differently and who have special needs. If the school does not have enough teachers and staff, it can be difficult to provide the necessary help for both regular and special learners. Some of the behavior characteristics of children with DS can cause teachers, other children, and parents to become upset.

Problems with behavior do not include only acting out, teasing, or hitting. A child with DS may allow himself or herself to be picked on by a bully or may be stubborn and refuse to follow directions. As is the case with any child, dealing with the situation thoughtfully and patiently usually helps.

What may seem like stubbornness in a child with DS may in fact be a persistent attempt to communicate. Likewise, what seems to be anger in the child with DS may be frustration at his or her own inability to learn or do something as quickly or as well as other students. Think about it: Don't you sometimes get angry when you are frustrated? The behavior of kids with DS becomes even easier to understand when they are included in all aspects of everyday life, especially in the classroom.

Chapter Four | Growing Up with DS

The school system really tries to help Joe. The bus he used to ride had a special harness to keep him safe. He outgrew that, yet he couldn't sit still. His horsing around distracted the driver and bothered the other kids, who made matters worse by teasing him.

The school took Joe off of the bus until the principal worked out a "circle of friends." Now these friends take turns sitting with him. They talk quietly and play games. Even though by law the school system had to meet his needs, Joe's parents feel that the school went out of its way to make the ride good for Joe, and good for the other students too.

Behavior Problems

Any child can be lovable, friendly, kind, selfish, angry, or bratty. This includes a child with DS. There is no behavior that is unique to children with DS. Because children with DS often are delayed in all stages of development, however, they may be older than the average child when they act a certain way. Most two-year-old children, for example, want their own way and do not like to share. For the child with DS, this stage may not be reached until he or she is older.

Like any other children, those with DS sometimes misbehave. The reason why is not always clear. For the child with DS, inappropriate behavior often is caused by a problem with focusing or by the desire to get his or her own way. Another frequent cause of misbehavior is frustration, caused by the inability to communicate with others. A little patience and understanding on the part of the listener can do much to minimize such frustration.

Problems Focusing

At times everyone finds it difficult to concentrate because of distractions. Children with DS may have a harder time blocking out distractions than most people. For example, a child with DS may find it difficult to pay attention in a classroom covered with bright posters and signs and mobiles that dangle from the ceiling. A student with DS is likely to find such a classroom cluttered and distracting, whereas for other students it simply might be stimulating.

Dealing with Misbehavior

My son is two and already is starting to throw things and not listen. He is developing more slowly than other children his age. We have an excellent doctor and a team of specialists—speech, physical therapy, and so on. They all seem to feel that most of this behavior is due to frustration over not being able to do the things he wants to do. He sees other children doing more than he can, and he wants to do those same things but just can't.

—A parent of a toddler with DS

Because many children with DS are delayed in their development, they often find it difficult to deal with the frustration of not getting their way. They also may see other children doing things that they would like to do and can become easily frustrated when they cannot.

The best way to deal with misbehavior by a child with DS is the same way you would deal with misbehavior by any child: Try to understand the reason for the misbehavior, and work with the child to find a way to keep it from happening again.

Sometimes particular actions seem "bad" because we do not understand why the person acted that way. Once the reason behind the action is understood, we see the behavior in a different light. Understanding the reason for behavior is not the same as tolerating behavior that is harmful or inappropriate.

Joel's teacher sent home a note that said that Joel had thrown a girl, Marie, to the floor. Of course, Marie was scared and upset. The teacher said that although Joel didn't seem angry, she, the girl, and the girl's parents couldn't understand his behavior. When Joel's mother questioned him about it, Joel looked puzzled. "Like Marie," he said. "Like her a lot."

In time, Joel's mother figured out that he had meant only to hug Marie. He had pushed her away so hard when he thought the hug should end that she had fallen on the floor. The incident was essentially an accident, not an example of anger or aggression. Once his mother understood why Joel had acted the way he did, his family and teacher were able to find a better way for Joel to interact with Marie.

Sometimes a task or lesson must be repeated over and over again before a young person with DS learns the best way of acting in a specific situation. Let's say an eight-year-old child with DS runs away from his parent in parking lots. A typical eight-year-old could be lectured or punished because he or she would be able to understand the possible dangerous consequences of this action. The child with DS, however, thinks more like a younger child. To stop the child from running away, the parent may have to hold his arm and make him walk from the car to the store and back, again and again, until he understands exactly what kind of behavior is expected.

The Same Standards

Parents, teachers, and friends should hold people with DS to the same standards as other people. Children with DS should understand that they cannot always get what they want or behave in whatever way suits them.

Maria wanted a new toy. Her mother said, "No, Maria. I do not have money to buy you a toy today. Besides, you got lots of toys last week for your birthday."

When they returned from the store, her mother noticed that Maria went quietly up to her bedroom and stayed there with the door closed for a long time. After a while, her mother peeked in. Maria was on her bed playing with a toy she had slipped into her pocket while they were in the store.

Her mother walked Maria back to the store and stood there while Maria gave the toy back and said she was sorry.

Exercise and Activities

A good long-term solution to a child's behavior problems often is to get him or her involved in a fun activity

Special Olympics is an international competition for developmentally challenged athletes.

that he or she can handle. Exercise is as important to the overall good health of people with DS as it is to everyone else, so children with DS should be encouraged to take part in a physical activity. If young people with DS can do so safely, they should be allowed to play whatever sports they enjoy.

Special Olympics

Special Olympics is a program that teaches and allows young people with mental retardation to take part in many different kinds of sports. Competitions are held at local, state, and national levels. Over one million athletes in nearly 150 countries and all fifty states in the United States train and compete.

For many children with DS and other developmental delays, joining Special Olympics is a good way to spend their time and take part in athletic activity and competition. As the Special Olympics Oath says, "Let me win. But if I cannot win, let me be brave in the attempt."

Community

Many people who use the term "inclusion" think of it as something that applies only to school. For people with DS, however, inclusion also means being included in events in the larger community where they live—for example, at a place of worship.

Today people with DS actively participate in social activities and community life.

Inclusion also means having a job, because in our world, money equals personal power. With a job that provides a paycheck, the person with DS can be independent to the greatest extent possible. That is the kind of power that most of us, including those with DS, want.

Giving Back to the Community

Some parents encourage their children with DS to visit nursing homes and to do community service work, with the idea that they give something back to the community. Such activities do serve the community, and they are a good idea for all teens, not just teens with DS. For those with DS, specifically, volunteer work can help make them feel like valuable members of the community and provide them with a good way to interact with other people.

Today's young adults with DS are, for the most part, the first students like them to attend school with both disabled and nondisabled students. They are the first to take an active part in community life and to benefit from some of the new research that has been done in recent years. What will their future be like?

Chapter Five

The Future for People with DS

When a child with DS becomes twenty-one, parents are hit with the reality that our kids will need care and support all their lives. This is where I am now.

—Rick Dill, parent

Because DS is not an illness, it cannot be outgrown. Because it is a genetic condition, nothing as yet can be done to prevent it. These two facts mean that babies will continue to be born with DS. Still, the outlook is better for people with DS than it has ever been. Why?

Improved Treatments

Advances in treatment and technology promise an improved life for those with DS. In the field of speech, for example, technology has created a generation of new equipment to assist people who have limited speech.

Advances in medicine also offer great hope. The search continues to find new uses for old drugs and to develop new medications. Because the life expectancy of people with DS is about ten years less than that of the average person, this area of research is extremely important.

Other advances in recent years—such as open-heart surgery, the development of ear tubes (for children with DS who suffer frequent ear infections), and new antibiotics—have done much to improve both the quality and the length of the lives of children with DS.

Lifelong Programs

New programs are opening doors for young people with DS that a few years ago would have stayed tightly shut. Lifelong programs improve the quality of life and allow adults with DS to hold a job, live in their own homes, and contribute to the community.

Most families pay—both in money and time—to provide for their child with DS, but they often find that extra support is needed from federal, state, and local governments. When they become older, adults with DS need extra help to live in a group home or other housing. They also may need support on a job and someone to at least oversee how well they take care of themselves, manage their money, spend their free time, and so on. Programs that provide these services cost a great deal of money.

"As parents we will not be around forever, and we probably will not have the resources to provide an assured comfortable life for our daughter with DS," Rick Dill points out. "We will have to depend upon the system to provide support, hopefully adequate, but not lavish."

It is little wonder that many parents of children with DS worry about funding their child's continuing care. Even though our laws now provide basic funding, any law, including IDEA, could be changed at any time. In addition, local and state funding for services for people with disabilities vary widely from one place in the United States to another, based mostly on the money an area collects in taxes and political and social priorities.

Despite ongoing concerns about money, most people feel that real growth has been made in programs to support people with DS throughout their lives. They point to the increased acceptance of people with DS as reason to believe that the future will be even brighter.

Public Acceptance and Inclusion

I want Katy to graduate with functional life skills. I want her exposed to a huge variety of real life and fun skills so that she can pick and choose what she's good at and what she wants to do.

—Amy Masser, mother of a child with DS

Acceptance in the workplace enables adults with DS to live successfully on their own.

Around the world, the trend is toward greater acceptance of the differences among people. Although many remain uncomfortable around people with disabilities, more and more people seem to feel that everyone, including those with disabilities, should be treated fairly.

The next step is to move from extending fair treatment to people with disabilities to true inclusion of those with disabilities as part of the community. People with DS will experience an even greater enjoyment of the huge variety of life experiences if the community can:

- Support funding that will help those with disabilities be successful and independent adults.

- Hire someone with DS, if the person can do the job.

- Try to accept and understand the special challenges of people with DS.

- Not discriminate in any way, especially on the basis of appearance.

- Support group homes and apartments in their neighborhoods so that those with disabilities can live independently outside their own family and feel like a welcome part of the community.

Why Change Is Slow

Bill loved his job cleaning tables at McDonald's. Still, he wondered why some people didn't seem to realize that he had feelings that could be hurt. One man yelled at him, "Hey, sped, hurry up and clean off this table."

A man at the next table said, "Hey, man, he's trying. Leave him alone."

Many adults are not open to having people with disabilities live on their street. They do not want to wait while a person with a disability slowly counts their money at a store. They are annoyed when someone has trouble understanding what they say. They laugh and tell jokes about people with problems.

As recently as twenty years ago, when these adults were growing up, those with disabilities such as DS were kept away from the general public. No wonder most adults don't feel comfortable around people with DS! They do not know how to interact with people with DS, and they don't feel comfortable doing so.

Are things different for people who have gone to school where those with disabilities were included? Sadly, many people with DS still seem to experience an increased sense of isolation as they grow older.

Although inclusion seems to work while children are young, most young people go their own way in their teens. Children with DS often find themselves more and more isolated and alone as they become young adults. Many parents of children with DS find that regardless of whether their children have been part of inclusion programs in school, they are likely to become increasingly isolated from the ages of thirteen to twenty-one. Inclusion at these ages seems to be forced or token. This is something parents have to recognize and deal with.

Most parents of children with DS find their child's isolation frustrating and work to keep their child involved in community life. After all, people with DS have the same feelings, drives, and urges that most everyone has. They want to go to school parties and dances, join clubs and community groups, and do everything that other young adults do. They want to have friends as well as boyfriends and girlfriends. This leads to all the usual concerns about sexual behavior, including the dangers of sexually transmitted diseases and unwanted pregnancy. These risks may be even greater for children with DS if they lack the necessary social skills to successfully negotiate potentially risky situations. The need for friendship, acceptance, and intimacy, combined with difficulty in communicating and setting boundaries, can make romantic and sexual relationships especially troublesome for teens with DS.

Most parents of adult children with DS understand

People with DS enjoy dating and relationships, just like everyone else.

that their children have sexual needs and desires. But pregnancy, in particular, is a great concern. Many parents of children with DS feel that the problems that might result from their child having and rearing his or her own children are simply too great to justify the risk. According to the National Association for Down Syndrome (NADS), there is only one documented case of a man with DS fathering a child. Women with DS can have children, but the child has a 35 to 50 percent chance of being born with DS. For these reasons many parents advise young adults with DS not to have children. Generally, parents of children with DS tend to be more concerned that their child lead a happy, full, independent life, where he or she will be accepted as a full member of the community, than with whether he or she has children or not.

No one with DS, child or adult, should live a life of isolation. If people are willing to allow them into their lives, a life apart easily can be turned into a life of inclusion.

Chapter Six | Down Syndrome Up Close

*T*he group home counselor sat with three young adults with DS at a table in the middle of the fast-food restaurant. She watched as other young people, just out of school and eager to eat, headed toward the empty seats near their table, looked at the four of them, and then moved to a table across the restaurant. She put down her burger and sighed.

Many of us keep our distance from someone who looks and seems different from ourselves and our friends. We move away from a table at which we see people who look different. At work or at school, we prefer to interact with those we know rather than someone whom we think is not like us. If you hesitate to interact with someone with DS, this chapter is aimed at you.

What We Say Matters

The way that we talk about other people matters. It surely matters to them. The way people talk about you matters to you, doesn't it? People with disabilities, including people with DS, are no less sensitive. Using the wrong words can cause a person and his or her family a lot of pain.

The words should also matter to us; they reflect our own feelings. Think of the word "handicapped." When that word is used to describe someone, does it cause you to expect less of him or her, or to think of him or her as less able to do a job than you would be? Many people think this way.

What some people say about people with DS often reflects a negative attitude toward them. "Idiot" is a term first used as one of scorn and abuse by the ancient Greeks. It later came to mean someone who was considered to be mentally "slow"—not particularly bright, "dimwitted," or "retarded." None of these terms should be used today, particularly to describe a person with a disability or DS. Neither should other derogatory terms that were once commonly used, such as "sped." Do some of your classmates seem to be unsure of how to refer to a fellow student with DS? Recommend that they try using his or her name.

If our words can show how little we think of someone, our respect for people with problems also can be shown by the words we use. How should we talk about, and to, a person with DS?

53

The Best Words to Use

Think of someone with DS as a person first, then as someone with DS. The best way to refer to someone with DS—or to anyone with a problem—is to put the person before the disability. By doing this you show that you think of him or her first and foremost as a person.

For example, you would not say, "Sure, I know that red-shirted kid." You would say, "Sure, I know that kid wearing a red shirt." So you should say, "Sure, I know that kid with DS." Better yet, find out the name of that kid with DS—and use it.

More Alike Than Different

Joan stood in the checkout line with Richie, her twelve-year-old son with DS. The cashier counted out Joan's change and said, "Ten dollars and one cent."

"Too much. Dime, not penny."

"Goodness, I did give your mom the wrong change!" said the cashier. She looked at Joan and smiled. "It's wonderful that he caught that. Just like a real person."

The woman at the checkout counter thought she was paying Richie a compliment, but she really was not. Her intentions might have been good, but she hadn't given what she said much thought. If asked, could she have listed any reasons why a person with DS was something other than a "real person"? Note that throughout this book you've read "child with DS," not "DS child." People with DS are real people—as real as anyone else.

How to Act and What to Say

Suppose you are watching your sister play soccer. A little boy with DS and his mother are standing next to you. The little boy smiles at you. He reaches into his pocket and takes out a pack of gum. He says, "Gum," and holds a stick in his hand for you to take. Do you walk away? Take the gum? Say something to his mother? Tell the kid to leave you alone? Or say, "No, thanks, I'm watching the game"?

The best advice can be summed up in one sentence: Treat someone with DS (or any disability) as you would anyone else. You do not need to go out of your way to talk or interact with him or her. Just because a child has a disability does not mean that you should pay more attention to him or her. At the same time, be polite. Just because someone has a disability does not mean that you should pay less attention to him or her, either.

Polite, but Not Overly Friendly

Many people with DS try to become instant friends with others. Their families worry that they will become friends with someone who will hurt them in some way, take their money, or abuse them. They try to teach children with DS that talking to strangers is not a good idea, and they prefer that strangers not respond to their children too quickly or in a super-friendly way. If someone with DS tries to become too friendly, the best thing to do is what you would do with any stranger: Be polite, but not overly friendly.

So what can you say? To a toddler, you might say, "Do you like to watch that big yellow bird on television?" You might ask someone older, "What's your favorite TV show?" And you can say to anyone, "Isn't the warm weather wonderful? I sure hope it lasts."

What NOT to Say to Family

Family and friends of children with DS get tired of hearing people say things that although meant to be kind, often hurt. Here are a few of them:

- "I know someone who has DS, and he's so loveable." (This one is offensive in two ways. DS is not an illness, like the flu, that someone has for a while and will get over. It is better to say that you know someone *with* DS. And loveable is not how people with DS always are.)

- "They're really sweet kids, aren't they?" (Well, not always.)

- "He'll be all right." (He's all right now, the way he is, and he won't get over being born with DS.)

- "She looks like she has just a little Downs." (If she was born with that extra chromosome,

she has DS; it is not a disease in which someone has a bad case *or* a mild case.)

Here are some things you can say or do:

- ◆ "I'm going to play catch with my sister. Can your son play too?" (This one is a little tricky. It assumes that the child is small and would need a parent's permission to play. If the child is older, you could talk directly to him.)

- ◆ If you know the child, simply say, "Hello." (If he or she is with a parent, explain that you know the child from school, or Little League, etc.)

- ◆ "Wow! What pretty blue eyes she has!"

In other words, your comments should say something about the child as an individual person. Treat the
person with DS as you would anyone else—as an individual deserving of respect.

What is the best way to do that? Include the person
with DS: Sit with him or her at lunch; bring the person into your conversations with other friends. Say
hello when you see him or her at school or other
places. Call him or her up some time, even if it is
simply to say hi. Treat a person with DS the same
way that you would treat anyone else—the way that
you would like to be treated.

Glossary

annual review   A yearly meeting to go over the Individualized Educational Plan (IEP).

assessment   Testing of a student to decide if there is a need for special education services.

developmental delay (mental retardation) Characterized from birth or infancy by intellectual ability that is severely below average.

epilepsy   Name for various disorders characterized by disturbances in the central nervous system that result in seizures and convulsions.

genetic (or hereditary) conditions   Specific conditions, syndromes, or diseases directly attributable to a child's genetic inheritance from his or her biological parents.

home schooling   Schooling that takes place exclusively in the home rather than in a school, usually under the direction of a parent.

IDEA Abbreviation for Individuals with Disabilities Education Act.

IEP Abbreviation for Individualized Educational Plan.

inclusion Education of a student with special needs in a general-education classroom.

ITP Abbreviation for Individualized Training Program; similar to the IEP, but spells out specifically what is needed to provide adult work and living skills.

PL94-142 Abbreviation for Public Law 94-142, which was the first legislation in the United States that provided for the public education of all children with disabilities.

self-contained class A special classroom, usually within a school building, where students with special needs spend most of the school day.

special services Services other than educational ones for a person who has been assessed and found to need those services. Examples include speech and language therapy, occupational therapy, physical therapy, and other forms of social work.

speech pathologist A person who is trained to work with people who have problems with speech and/or language. A speech pathologist might help a person who is speech impaired find different ways to communicate with others as well as improve his or her speech.

Where to Go for Help

ARC
500 East Border Street, Suite 300
Arlington, TX 76010
(800) 433-5255
TTY: (817) 277-0553
Web site: http://thearc.org/welcome.html
This is a well-known and respected organization, formerly known as the Association of Retarded Citizens.

Council for Exceptional Children
1920 Association Drive
Reston, VA 20191
(888) 232-7733
Web site: http://www.cec.sped.org
This international professional association of special educators develops programs for people with special needs. Web pages are updated weekly with current news about special education.

Jan Dill
Web site: http://www.cyburban.com/~rdill/jan1.html
This site describes the life of Dill, a young woman with DS.

Len Leshin, M.D., F.A.A.P.
Web site: http://ds-health.com
Dr. Leshin is the father of a child with DS. His Web site has a lot of good information and links, including a special page for students writing reports on DS.

National Down's Syndrome Congress
1605 Chantilly Drive, Suite 250
Atlanta, GA 30324
(800) 232-6372
Web site: http://www.carol.net/~ndsc

National Down Syndrome Society
666 Broadway, Suite 810
New York, NY 10012
(800) 221-4602
Web site: http://ndss.org
The National Down Syndrome Society supports DS research; provides basic information about DS; and also lists books, videos, and other materials.

Special Olympics
Web site: http://www.specialolympics.org
Special Olympics is an international organization that trains developmentally challenged children to take part and compete in athletic activities.

For Further Reading

Anderson, W., S. Chitwood, and D. Hayden. *Negotiating the Special Education Maze: A Guide for Parents and Teachers.* Reston, VA: Council for Exceptional Children, 1997.

Bowman-Kruhm, Mary, and Claudine Wirths. *Coping with Discrimination and Prejudice.* New York: Rosen Publishing Group, 1998.

Selikowitz, M. *Down Syndrome: The Facts.* New York: Oxford University Press, 1997.

Westridge Young Writers Workshop. *Kids Explore the Gifts of Children with Special Needs.* Santa Fe, NM: John Muir Publications, 1994.

Index

Index

About the Author

Dr. Mary Bowman-Kruhm is a writer and educator. She is the author of more than twenty books for teens, as well as numerous articles for professional journals and magazines.

Photo Credits

Cover and pp. 2, 41, 46 © Greenlar/The Image Works; p. 13 © Custom Medical Stock Photo; p. 15 © Biophoto Associates/Science Source; pp. 24, 32 © Sean O'Brien/Custom Medical Stock Photo; pp. 19, 21, 39 © Lawrence Migdale/Photo Researchers, Inc.; p. 29 © Richard Hutchings/Photo Researcher, Inc.; p. 8 © Ron Chapple/FPG International; p. 50 © Michael L. Palmieri/The Ames Tribune.

Design and Layout

Annie O'Donnell